SIZES

Carol Watson
Illustrated by David Higham
Consultant: Wyn Brooks
Deputy-Head Teacher of The Coombes School,
Arborfield, Berkshire; lectures widely on
Primary School Mathematics.

Farmer Jo has lots of animals.

They are all different sizes.

The carthorse is bigger than the bull

Which is the biggest animal?

The bull is bigger than the cow.

Which is the smallest?

The sheep is fatter than the dog.
The pig is fatter than the sheep.

Which is the fattest?
Which is the thinnest?

A lamb is a small animal.

But a lamb is bigger

than a cat,
which is bigger

than a rat,
which is bigger

than a mouse.

Which is the smallest?

Three farmhands help Farmer Jo.

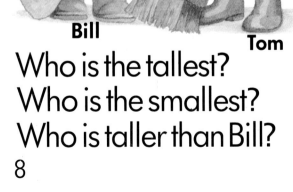

Bill

Tom

Jim

Who is the tallest?
Who is the smallest?
Who is taller than Bill?

They use a pitchfork, a spade and a brush.

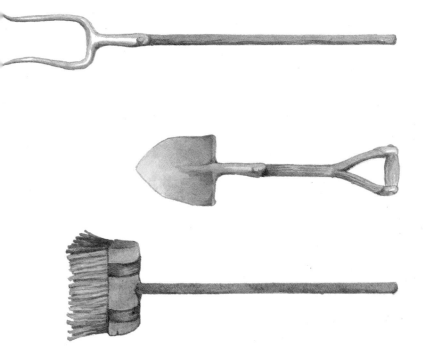

Which is the shortest?
Which is the longest?
Which one is longer than the brush?

Farmer Jo is driving his tractor out of the barn.

The door is wide.

Poor Daisy is stuck in the door
of the cowshed.

The door is narrow.

Farmer Jo wants to know the size of his farmyard.

He and his friends are measuring. You can measure with your body.

a span

a footstep

You can measure with a ruler or tape-measure.

How many of Jim's footsteps will it

Jim's boots

How many of Tom's footsteps will it

Tom's boots

How many of Bill's footsteps will it

Bill's boots

Who do you think took the most footsteps? Why?

14

ake to reach the bucket?

ake to reach the bucket?

ake to reach the bucket?

It is milking time for Farmer Jo's cows.

Daisy

Which cow has given the most milk

Which has given the least?

The farmer's wife gives some milk
to Tom, Jim and Bill.

She gives them each the same
amount.

Tom thinks he has got more than
the other two. Has he?

Why does he think that?
What is different about the bottles?

Jim, Bill and Tom have been picking apples.

Who do you think has the most apples? Who has the least?

The farmer's wife is making a pie.

Which holds the most flour — the cup, the bowl or the tin?

Bill, Jim and Tom are mending the fence. They each have a piece of wood.

Who has the biggest piece, or are they the same size?

Use the squares to help you find out.

Puzzle picture
The farmhands have got their boots mixed up.

Which boots belong to which feet?

First published in 1983
Usborne Publishing Ltd
20 Garrick St London
WC2 9BJ, England
© Usborne Publishing Ltd 1983

The name of Usborne and the device 🎈 are Trade Marks of Usborne Publishing Ltd.
Printed in Belgium by Casterman S.A.